THE POLITICALLY INCORRECT DICTIONARY FOR THE '90s

To Karin,

with best wishes

Greg Dahl.

The Politically Incorrect Dictionary For The 90s

P.O. BOX 54, Station "F",
TORONTO, ONTARIO M4Y 2L5
CANADA

ISNB 0-9699240-0-3

In Memory of
Christopher Lailey ffolkes Jemmett
1943-1994

EDITORS

Barbara Storrison
Christopher Wright
David Ikeda
Daphne Cuthill
Eleanor Hooks
June Lamb
Marc Medhi Taslimi
Marg Connor
Miguel Ramos
Patrick Rabbitskin
Patricia Berger
Patricia Creed
Paul Hill
Peggy Barrick
Pierre P. La Traverse
Shelagh Roberts
Sully Ramos
William D. Heintzman

Other work by GffW: SEVENTEEN-EIGHTEEN

Cover and illustration: Tom Nicholson
Layout: Simon Konatowicz

INTRODUCTION

Political correctness is a state where only the left are right. This book is a collection of observations at various ends of the spectrum. I hope that this book encourages the reader to lighten up. The purpose of the booklet/booklette was to comment on the serious, the tiresome, and the ridiculous.

It seems only right that I acknowledge Ambrose Bierce whose collection of thoughts from the turn of the century formed ''The Devils Dictionary''.

Thanks to friends and family who have encouraged me and offered advice particularly Patsy Walsh who provided very valuable information and reference materials.

There were a number of friends who assisted me in editing this work for which I thank them. Their knowledge of grammar and punctuation have clarified many points. Their greater contribution was to determine what makes sense to the reader.

Gregory ffolkes Walsh

January 1995 Toronto, Ontario

A

Abortion A political issue on which too many men have an opinion.

Accomplishment Innate talent when seen in oneself, a result of luck when seen in others.

Accountant A magician who can demonstrate that liabilities are assets.

Acquaintance Someone not worth knowing well.

Acronym The efficient language of exclusion.

Adult Legally, an artificial measurement when one is more accountable than one was the day before.

Aging Chronologically challenged.

Agnostic One who argues strongly for something he doesn't believe in.

AIDS A health issue some people confuse with a moral issue.

Alcoholic One who appreciates nature's fruit more than nature itself.

Alimony A system which demonstrates two do not live as cheaply as one.

Ancestor A shadow of one's former self.

Anger An emotion demonstrated when someone does not fulfil your expectations of how s/he should have behaved.

Anonymous Not surprisingly, the author of many religious hymns.

Art The skill to form available materials into an expression of oneself.

Atrocity New York City: a description of a city gone wrong.

Autocrat One who is intolerant of back seat drivers.

Autobiography The opportunity to dispel myths with lies.

B

Backbencher A member of a legislature with only local appeal and an even narrower focus.

Bailiff One who has a better understanding of human frailty and greed than the preacher.

Bank An institution that offers you money when you don't need it and asks for repayment when you are unable to do so.

Barter An environmentally more friendly transaction.

Bilingual Having the capacity to be misunderstood in two languages.

Binge An adolescent measurement of capacity, volume, and time.

Abortion A political issue on which too many men have an opinion.

Biological Being of two minds.

Birth The beginning of the end.

Blues An art form where ones' misery is put to song.

Bobbitt affair The Where the phrase "a bird in the hand" means you are in serious trouble.

Born-again Christian One who has a childlike understanding of scripture.

Breakfast One of the more consistent reasons why many people bother to get up in the morning.

Bureaucracy What can be said that hasn't been said already.

C

Capital punishment A weekend in Ottawa.

Capitalism A system that favours the clever, dishonest, and privileged; common in all other systems.

Career A job with meaning.

Catholic Salvation by birth.

Central committee The suppository of all knowledge.

Certainty The expedient method of excluding probabilities.

Christmas An event where one wishes that Jesus had a sibling, so that we can doubly enjoy the event.

Church collection The tithe that binds.

Civil servant Neither.

Cocaine Once the purview of rich and artistic fools, now cheaper versions make it affordable to any fool.

Commandment As in the Old Testament: Thou shall not covet thy neighbour's wife or ass.

Comment An opinion without consequence.

Committee The longest distance between two points.

Commitment Something easily given when one sees the end result, an admirable quality in someone who acts on faith alone.

Common law Once rare, now common.

Compromise The middle point between realism and idealism.

Computer A device that accelerates the margin of human error.

Condom A product that, according to some, rubber stamps promiscuity.

Confession The penicillin for sin.

Consolation To experience the relief that a misfortune did not happen to you.

Conscience Having second thoughts.

Conservative One who believes in the divine right of individual freedom, usually at the cost of those less divine.

Born-again Christian One who has a childlike understanding of scripture.

Consensus Determining a means to an end when no clear option is evident.

Consultant An unemployed person with a business card.

Contract A signed agreement among parties who do not trust each other's word.

Country music A repetitive art form causing involuntary foot movement in even the most sophisticated.

Creativity A recognized ability to transform one's ideas to another's liking.

Credit card A symbolic facsimile of security and wealth.

Cremation Makes resurrection as a possibility seem less likely.

Cross border shopping A method supporting the theory that if the American economy is booming so too will Canada's.

Crusade Historically an evil done under the guise of good.

Cryonics If at first you don't succeed..

Cult An earthly paradise for lost souls.

Customer service Clearly evidenced in banks which have us believe that one long line provides better service than five short lines.

D

Date rape Violence with a name, where fools think familiarity breeds consent.

Day care A place where children depend on the kindness of strangers.

Depression A state of mind affecting only those capable of thought.

Designer (clothes) A garment where the name is of greater value than the costume.

Designer (interior) One who puts on airs.

Designer (exterior) One who puts on facades.

Designer (genes) Once a way of making a statement through the quality of clothes you wear, now becomes a way of making a statement through the quality of offspring you can produce.

Designated driver Measured sanity.

Desire An unattained satisfaction, increasingly fueled by each satisfier.

Destiny The next exit.

Dictionary The unreliable reference in the English language for determining how to spell a word.

Diet A reactive excess to previous excesses.

Dissatisfaction Ambition's motivator.

Divorce court The house of ill dispute.

Dolphin A mammal, which if it were as smart as people say, should know better than to swim with tuna.

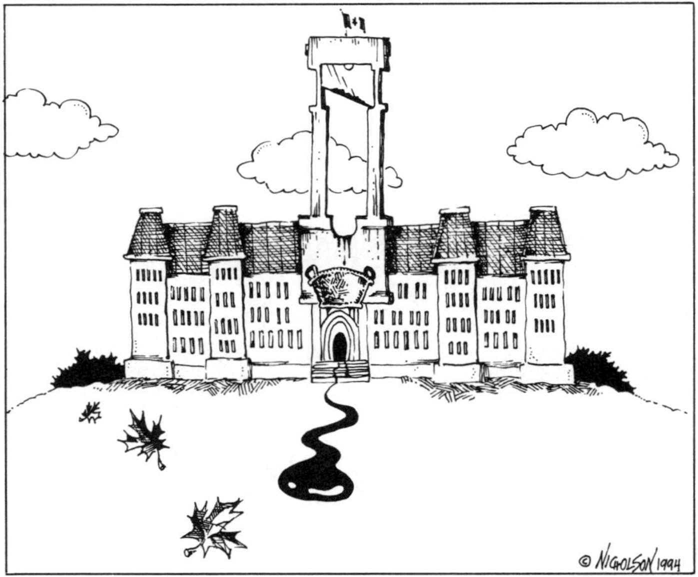

Capital punishment A weekend in Ottawa.

Downpayment The initial step to debt.

Downsizing Making the horses leave so you can close the barn door.

E

Eccentricity A tolerable madness.

Economist One whose forecasts make weather forecasts look reliable.

Election An environmentally compatible endeavour to reduce, recycle, and reuse political promises.

Eligible bachelor If that were truly so, he wouldn't be eligible.

Elitist One who surrounds oneself with inferiors.

Emotion The only part of the human mind that becomes less flexible when exercised too often.

Employment A measurement by which people judge your value or worth.

Employment equity Legislation designed to ensure that all workers are equally undervalued.

Empowerment The illusion of having some control in our lives.

Environmental disaster Like a slow lingering death it has the same end result as a sudden death.

Environmentalist One whose convictions attack the producers but rarely the consumers.

Equalizer Traffic jams, flight delays, death, pollution.

Estimate The lowest common denominator of potential price.

Eternity An everlasting concept most clearly understood when waiting for someone.

Excuse The first cousin of failure.

Expert A vanishing breed in future organizations.

Explanation The provision of information to others who were too lazy to find out for themselves.

Euthanasia The issue that focuses on quality rather than quantity.

Evolution A higher species is separated from a lower species by it's ability to accessorize.

Evolution A higher species is separated from a lower species by it's ability to accessorize.

F

Faith Bungee jumping, driving in Montreal, buying second hand.

Family (dysfunctional) The unit blamed if you are screwed up.

Family (functional) If you are screwed up you have no one to blame but yourself.

Fishing A Canadian industry best pursued in Portugal.

Flattery A statement received graciously, no matter how embellished or untrue.

Forgiveness People are forgiven, but their names not forgotten.

Forms The cobwebs of bureaucracy.

Fortune teller Forbes magazine's annual list.

Fox hunting A sport developed by the Royals when they could no longer hunt down the lower classes.

Free speech Often free advertising to bad ideas.

Free trade An economic plan to shift profit from manufacturers to distributors.

Friend In America, anyone who has been introduced and remembered. In England, someone of the same class who has been tolerated for 40 years.

Fundamentalism In religion where God is always right and its followers more right.

Funeral Proof that the debts men incur live after them.

Fur coat A politically unacceptable article except when is made from a road kill.

Future The vague hope that there is an extension of the present good.

G

Garden party An event often held by people who live in small houses.

Gardening A mundane job; an even more mundane hobby.

Gasoline The cheapest litre of liquid on the market save water, yet the most costly to produce.

Gay To some the ultimate form of male bonding, to others the ultimate in mal-bonding.

General delivery To be of no fixed address.

Genius A higher intellect, curiously in the masculine form. The female is thought to be a genie.

Generalization In the avoidance of specificity, a method of communication to better be understood by others equally ignorant of the subject.

Genius A higher intellect, curiously in the masculine form. The female is thought to be a genie.

Germany A country of two minds and pocketbooks.

Gerontophile One who pursues the company of elders.

Glad A state of joy for a realist.

Gold A mineral that reinforces man's obsession with the value of the abstract.

Gossip A communicable disease.

Green with envy Inexperienced jealousy.

Ground hog Saddam Hussein.

H

Half-assed Contrary to the Protestant ethic, a more Christian approach of turning the other cheek.

Happiness An experience only felt in the present tense.

Hairdresser The one who hears more confessions than a priest but never dispenses penance, other than a bad perm.

Hate The expression of innate inferiority.

Heartache Unlike heartburn which results from an excess of eating, heartache is from an excess of expectations.

Heimlich manoeuvre Not to be confused with the Hindlick manoeuvre of kissing up to the boss.

Heredity Only spoken of when one takes credit for his/her ancestors.

Heresy When one's opinion is more than wrong.

Hindsight Those who espouse the value of hindsight really believe they do have eyes in the back of their head.

History To have the benefit of judgement knowing both the action and result.

Honesty A self-indulgent opinion of truth.

Human Rights Commission A body established where rights are valued most and abuses occur least.

Humility A covert concession of the fact that others will never fully understand your talents.

Hunting The logic of hunting as a sport makes war appear sensible.

I

Idea A reaction that occasionally turns to action.

Identity The ability to not only recognize oneself in a mirror, but to accept it as well.

Identity crisis The convergence of illusion and delusion.

Ideology The weakest link in a society.

Ignorant Describes anyone who lacks your knowledge or experience.

Immigrant An immigrant is a person who has a strange accent. An emigrant just has a different English accent.

Immortality Only words and deeds achieve immortality. The illusion that individuals achieve it results in words and deeds.

Klu Klux Klan A shy group of cross dressers.

Incest A familiar form of sexual assault.

Inclusion A political catch phrase that means we want to have you involved as long as you play by our rules,and only our rules.

Indigenous In the Americas: impoverished.

Indulgence The relaxation of denial.

Infidelity To be out of harmony.

Infinity A temporal word defined by the first migraine sufferer.

Information superhighway Confusion at a break-neck pace; where absolute information confuses absolutely.

Iron Man A challenging rediscovery that separates the boys from the boys.

J

Job stress reduction A pink slip.

Jogging A middle class exercise where distance has greater value than destination and the means justify the end.

Joke Usually an amusing tale told at someone else's expense.

Journalist One who presents his/her view as fact.

K

Klu Klux Klan A shy group of cross dressers.

Kindness A human interaction noted usually because of it's rarity.

L

Latter Day Saint A pious night person.

Lawyer A professional who profits himself only.

Legal system A logical structure to limit the excesses of individual liberties, not to be confused with justice.

Lesbian A womyn in comfortable shoes.

Level playing field Where two warring parties are not equal; but are armed equally, at least providing an illusion of equality.

Libation A formal slug of wine.

Liberal A political philosophy that presumes there is always a better way.

Information superhighway Confusion at a break-neck pace; where absolute information confuses absolutely.

Liberty The capacity to choose ones' own chains.

Library science An efficient method to locate books. If it were an art, libraries would only have books worth reading.

Life insurance Betting against the inevitable.

Liquor The most acceptable harmful substance in the world.

Literacy A skill required to read The Globe & Mail, but not the Toronto Sun.

Little woman An unusually diminutive phrase used in previous generations by diminutive men when describing their wives.

Logging A traditional Canadian industry that becomes less traditional as people discover how long it takes a 200 year old tree to become a renewable resource.

Loneliness A self-inflicted state best enjoyed when shared.

Lost in thought A state that describes familiar territory for a politician.

Lotteries Government's tax on avarice.

Love An implausible state usually taken for granted when achieved and valued only when lost.

Luck The result of positioning time, space and opportunity correctly.

M

Madame A chargé d'affaires.

Mankind An ancient form of civilization that was replaced by human kind around 1980, an abler people.

Maple Leaf A Canadian symbol that looks best in its dying state.

Marriage The conclusion of man's search for the perfect woman and woman's search for the imperfect man.

Marx-Engels An economic system now being replaced with the more modern one of Marks and Spencer.

Master bedroom Now simply referred to as the main bedroom.

Metric A measurement that assures greater accuracy of error.

Menopause A female liberation of cyclical drudgery.

Midwife A woman engaged.

Militant One who puts principles ahead of people.

Morality A set of principles that changes with each circumstance.

Movie A film or video longer than 60 minutes.

Multiculturalism A Canadian political policy that promotes our differences instead of our similarities.

Life insurance Betting against the inevitable.

Mutual fund A group of piggies going to market.

Mutually exclusive A duel where both antagonists lose.

N

Narcoleptic One who has an overwhelming desire to kidnap an undercover cop.

Native self-government An illusionary concept to redress 200 years of discrimination.

Neo-nazism A forum to channel hatred.

Networking In business, a form of mutually beneficial self promotion.

Neutral A safe position to be in, but only on a level playing field.

New Democrat A political party best governing in opposition.

Non conformist In principles, a radical admired; in mentality, one scorned.

O

Open mind A description of a reasonable person lacking conviction.

Opera A tragedy that is linguistically removed from reality.

Outdoors The only truly designated smoking area in Toronto.

Oxymoron A dumb ass.

Ozone layer A nebulous film further being depleted by massive emissions of sun tan spray.

P

Paradigm For some, a subjective view of reality; for others, twenty cents.

Paranoid Having some knowledge of reality.

Partnership A relationship where a dominant party convinces the other that they are equal.

Patriotism An opportunity to die for the abstract.

Person A generic being of either sex for whom a label would be inappropriate in all cases.

Personality The ability to demonstrate style over substance.

Love An implausible state usually taken for granted when achieved and valued only when lost.

Pessimism Every silver lining has a cloud.

Pet peeve A personal and regular annoyance of your neighbour's cat.

Philosophy Most of us follow the tenets of confusionism.

Philanthropist One who uses another's hard spent money in his name for the benefit of others.

Phone sex Technology's answer to sexually transmitted diseases.

Pimp An agent who needs no skills and gets a commission for someone else's work.

Plagiarize To appreciate the work of another more fully than was intended.

Plastic surgery A medical procedure for plastic people.

Poet A lyricist who cannot sing.

Politics The art of muddle over matter.

Politically correct A process whereby group rights supersede those of individuals.

Pollster One who determines the best way to form a question to elicit an expected response.

Polyester Politically correct material, except in an oil shortage.

Pompous To embellish circumstance.

Poverty A malady defined and measured by its relative environment.

Power lunch A digestion of decisions.

Prediction A circumstance which, in hindsight, everyone expected but for which no one prepared.

Prime Minister More appropriately a name for the Pope, as most Prime Ministers act as if they were infallible.

Private club An organization which discriminates exclusively.

Procrastinate To... To... To...

Profession An employment where one has determined the fastest rate of return on one's academic investment.

Project A collection of tasks with a defined end, but often with no purpose.

Promiscuous Someone who has sex more often than you.

Prompt Can mean earlier than expected, but not necessarily on time.

Prophet One who guesses with greater than 50 percent accuracy.

Province An area that defines a Canadian.

Psychology The science of presumption used to determine another's motivation.

Punk Primitive, Underground, Narcissistic Kid.

Outdoors The only truly designated smoking area in Toronto.

Q

Quality Time A Cartier watch.

Quintessential Touch, hear, smell, see, taste.

R

Radical An opinion stridently articulated by opposite poles. The centrist knows both poles are wrong, the far left and far right only know that the other is wrong.

Rectory In the Catholic sphere; a home for unwed fathers.

Redeployment In government, a transfer of unwilling staff.

Reform Party politics A return to a simpler way of life where simple logic covers the complexity of reality.

Religion Something that provides comfort to the uncomfortable.

Reorgs An abbreviation: reusable body parts.

Reputation A good reputation is easily lost, a bad one easily attained.

Responsibility A trait expected of others in greater measure than in oneself.

Retrograde Today's version of regular gasoline.

Reunion An opportunity to relive both the joys and insecurities of youth.

Review A long-winded opinion of movies, usually by one who has never produced, directed or acted.

Romance novel Stories with template plots.

Royal Commission So called, as most reign longer than monarchs.

Royal Family A family similar to most families. However, when it screws up, it does it royally.

Rules A system developed to stifle judgement.

Phone sex Technology's answer to sexually transmitted diseases.

S

Sale An event where items are charged nearer to their true value.

Santa Claus A jolly figure with a corncob pipe used by the tobacco industry to encourage children to smoke.

Sauna Allows the idle to feel a sense of achievement by the sweat of their brow.

Scandal A known transgression that is a disaster to oneself, but advantageous when it affects another.

Scepticism The productive cousin of cynicism.

Science The singular state that exists when people reach agreement.

Secret A shared experience/knowledge once told is no longer.

Self confidence The most common ingredient of error.

Self determination A state that minorities seek, but is granted only by the majority.

Self doubt For some, an aphrodisiac to accomplishment.

Self esteem The fundamental ingredient for balanced individualism.

Self-help book Literature designed for people who cannot help themselves.

Self-made-man The only one known was the result of the Immaculate Conception.

Semi-detached An emotionally involved WASP.

Shelter (Men's) A place of refuge from the world.

Shelter (Women's) A place of refuge from men.

Signature The only abstract with consequence.

Sin tax Government's pre-penance.

Slash The most important politically correct development in the English language: S/he,and/or... It allows the reader (him/her) to (read/not read) whatever (s/he) wants to (see/not see).

Smoking A marginally acceptable addiction pursued by people who know better.

Snob When viewed by a person of mediocrity, one who presumes equality.

Social workers People who believe in the frailty of the human spirit.

Spousal benefits A legal symbolism of the status quo.

Statistics If truth were self-evident, statistics would be unnecessary.

Stud A person whose image exceeds his substance.

Sun tan Once the mark of a servant in the fields, more recently of the idle rich and now of the fool.

T

Talk shows Television programming that allow the average person to believe s/he is normal.

Teacher One who is charged to give children all the moral, religious, health, and social upbringing that parents, churches, and others are no longer prepared to give.

Telemarketing In the extreme case, a computer trying to sell a product or service to an answering machine.

Telephone directory A rarely used and wasteful publication that is inaccurate upon each printing.

Television news The highest form of stylized presentation.

Terrorist One who uses explosives to demonstrate his powerlessness.

"They say" The most quoted source of authority when the true source is unavailable.

Thought A process activated when one is inactive.

Tolerance The ability to accept anything that is of little personal consequence.

Toronto The most cosmopolitan city east of Mississauga.

Tourist A traveller in purgatory; a country's penance for it's beauty.

Treachery A clever action that produces a loser.

Poverty A malady defined and measured by its relative environment.

Trust The investment required for risk.

Truth Something on which an opinion should not be formed.

TV evangelist Proof that "a man's greed must exceed his grasp, or what's a heaven for?"

U

Underachievement The result of setting unrealistic goals.

Underground economy Once the economy of natural resources, but now the economy of unnatural resourcefulness.

Union An association of employees whose elected leaders often espouse the doctrines which they were elected to oppose.

United Kingdom Four separate and distinct national groups under the titular rule of a queen.

V

Vanity To be unencumbered with self doubt.

Vegetable An edible ugly flower.

Vegetarian One who consciously works himself into a lather over leather.

Verdicts Judgements when people confuse not guilty with innocence.

Victim The one forgotten in the pursuit of justice and individual rights.

Virtual reality The economic system.

Visual media The greatest supporter of illiteracy.

Visible Minority An urban misnomer and a rural rarity. In politics, voters should be seen but not heard.

Volunteer Demonstrates that even menial labour has value when one is not paid for it.

W

War An event which always ends for better reasons than it starts.

Wealth A state where one lacking in want achieves easily.

Weather report An excellent way to learn about geography, but not climate.

Welfare To fare marginally, but not well.

White collar crime White collars study crime and consider the act an exception. Blue collar crime has no descriptive.

Wine A product that makes disagreeable people more tolerable.

Womyn A politically correct gender.

Womens liberation A western movement that focuses on man's injustice to middle class women; yet allows women to have a career plus do housework and rear children.

Y

Yellow pages Along with black magic and white pages, an unacceptable colour description.

Young Offenders Act But not very well.

Z

Zoo If people were an endangered species, the most vulnerable would have at least three meals a day and a roof over their head.

The Author

Gregory ffolkes Walsh
is a refugee from Montreal who now resides in downtown Toronto. He was educated at the University of Montreal and Concordia University.
Aside from working in the provincial civil service he volunteers with various youth and social service agencies.

This is his second book.
The first "Seventeen-Eighteen" is out of print.

The Illustrator

Thomas J. Nicholson
is a freelance illustrator who resides in Toronto
with his son.
He strives to be apolitical and incorrect
as possible.
In his spare time he work as a janitor.

ORDER FORM

Please send me _____ copies of **The Politically Incorrect Dictionary For The 90s**.
Each copy is $12.95 (Cdn), plus $4.00 for shipping and handling.

Send cheque or money order (Canadian Funds) to:
BRANAGH PRESS
P.O. BOX 54, Station "F",
TORONTO, ONTARIO M4Y 2L5
CANADA

PLEASE PRINT:

SHIP TO:
Name ___________________________________
Address ______________________ Apt. ________
City ___________________ Prov/State ________
Postal Code ________ Country _______________